Author—John McKenzie, o.s.b.
Monastero di San Benedetto di Norcia
Via Reguardati; 22 - 06046 NORCIA (PG) Italy
librinursia@osbnorcia.org
www.osbnorcia.org

Illustrator—Mark Brown
663 2nd Street - Ayden NC, 28513 USA
mbrown3@artic.edu

Graphic Designer—Siobhan Royer
graylingstudio.com
design@graylingstudio.com

Under the direction of Romain Lizé, Vice President, MAGNIFICAT

Editor, MAGNIFICAT : Isabelle Galmiche
Editor, Ignatius: Vivian Dudro
Assistant of the Editor: Pascale Vandewalle
Layout Designer: Elena Germain
Production: Thierry Dubus, Sabine Marioni

Original edition: © 2013 by Citta Ideale, Prato.
Design by Siobhan Royer from Graylingstudio

John McKenzie, o.s.b. ✛ Mark Brown
Monastero di San Benedetto di Norcia

The Life of Saint Benedict

Magnificat · Ignatius

The Birth of Saints Benedict and Scholastica

Saints Benedict and Scholastica were twins born around A.D. 480, that is, more than one thousand five hundred years ago, in a small mountain town in Italy called Nursia. Their father, Euproprio, was a military officer of the legendary Roman Empire, sent to Nursia to calm a local rebellion. Their mother, Abbondanza, was from Nursia. The two were devout Christians and raised their children in the truths of the Catholic faith. They probably had no idea that their twins would one day become renowned saints and their son Benedict would become one of the most important figures in Christian history. Benedict founded many monasteries. He authored a way of life for monks that helped many people, both young and old, to grow in holiness. Monks who followed the Rule of Saint Benedict later became known as Benedictines. Today the Benedictines have monasteries throughout the entire world, and the monks or nuns who live in them come in all sorts of shapes, sizes, and colors.

This scene portrays the birth of the saintly twins. The location now forms part of a monastery, where the monks care for the birthplace of Benedict and Scholastica.

Pope Saint Gregory the Great

The life of Saint Benedict became known to the world by means of Pope Saint Gregory the Great, who, like Saint Benedict, was a monk. Only later in life did Gregory become the bishop of Rome, the pope. In the sixth century he wrote a four-volume book on the lives of different saints in Italy. Gregory thought Benedict's life was so important that he dedicated an entire volume to it. This scene shows Pope Gregory the Great dictating the life of Benedict to his disciple Peter the Deacon. The chair Gregory is sitting in is a faithful copy of the actual chair he used as pope. This chair is housed in the monastery that Gregory founded in Rome.

Nursia, the Birthplace of Saints Benedict and Scholastica

Nursia is a very ancient and beautiful town located in the Sibylline Mountains. It is known today for its tasty lentils and cheeses, and especially for its meats, such as wild boar! During the time of Benedict and Scholastica the Roman Empire was still quite pagan; nevertheless, in many places Christianity thrived and had a great influence on the people. At this time, many hermits and monks lived in the area of Nursia. Some were locals who desired to live a holier life, while others were foreigners who came to seek refuge because they were being persecuted in their own country due to their steadfast faith in Christ and his Church. Many of the hermitages and monastic dwellings exist to this day. In fact, there are still hermits and monks in the area.

Saints Benedict, Scholastica, Eutizio, and Fiorenzo Encounter the Saintly Abbot Spes

Up in the mountains not too far from the ancient town of Nursia is a beautiful monastery dedicated to Saints Spes and Eutizio. Saint Spes was the abbot of this monastery when Saint Benedict was still a boy. Abbot Spes was blind for about forty years of his life; however, just before he died the Lord appeared to him and asked him to preach at the different monasteries he had founded in the area. In order for him to do this, the Lord Jesus Christ gave him back his sight. Shortly after he finished with his preaching he passed away in the Lord.

In the illustration, we see Abbot Spes with the four children destined to become saints. In front of him are the young twins, Benedict and Scholastica. Fiorenzo is looking out toward the wilderness because he lived a great portion of his life as a hermit there, where he would spend hours on end in prayer to God. He even became friends with many of the animals he encountered while living in the forest. One of these animals was a wild bear who was faithful to him until the end.

Behind Saint Spes is Eutizio with a small staff. He later became abbot of the monastery sometime after the death of Spes. Eutizio was so eager to make Jesus better known that he spent a great portion of his time preaching the gospel to the people.

Saint Benedict Goes to Rome for Studies

Saint Benedict's parents sent him to Rome for studies when he was a teenager. His sister, Saint Gregory tells us, consecrated her life to God when she was a young girl. Soon Benedict would follow in the footsteps of his twin sister.

Saint Benedict in Rome

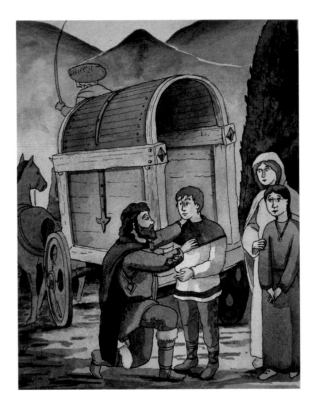

Saint Benedict had a difficult time during his studies in Rome. He had been raised in a very devout Christian family, but he soon came to learn that not everyone acts the way one should. Early on Benedict chose the way of virtue rather than that of vice. His time in Rome, though difficult, became a time for him to reflect about his choice in life. After witnessing all the evil around him, he decided to leave Rome in pursuit of a way to serve Christ and his Church.

This scene shows a young Benedict while at school. He attempts to concentrate on his studies while the other boys spend their time joking around.

Saint Benedict Flees to the Hills of Subiaco

Along with a faithful family servant who had helped to raise him, Benedict went to places near Rome in order to dedicate his life to prayer and penance. After a while, he left his nurse in order to live the solitary life in a cave outside Subiaco, a mountain village east of Rome.

The years of solitude served as a time of purification for the saint. He dressed in animal skins and grew a long beard. In fact shepherds sometimes confused him with a wild animal of some kind. During this time he made friends with a certain Saint Romanus, who lived in a monastery just above his cave. Romanus used to send bread down to Benedict by means of a basket on a rope. Later, Romanus clothed Benedict with the monastic habit. No longer would he be mistaken for a wild animal!

Saint Benedict Becomes Well Known

It did not take long for people to realize that the mysterious person they would see every so often was in fact a holy man. This scene depicts Benedict explaining the gospel to some of the locals, some of whom were shepherds. Many of them became so enthusiastic about following Christ that, by the grace of God, they sought to live the same life as Benedict lived. Saint Benedict's holiness and his knowledge of God prompted others to turn from their former ways to the ways of the Lord.

Saint Scholastica in Nursia

This scene shows Saint Scholastica receiving some of her neighbors and giving alms to a man in need. She lived not too far from the city of Nursia, in a villa owned by her family. Like her twin brother in the rugged cave of Subiaco, Scholastica dedicated much of her time to prayer and penance. Later on she would join her brother at the now-famous monastery of Monte Cassino.

Some Wicked Monks Ask Benedict to Be Their Abbot

This picture shows a band of monks who wanted Saint Benedict to become their abbot. At first Benedict refused their request, but after a time he agreed to be their leader. Soon afterward Benedict saw that their life and his were totally opposite. Benedict loved God so much that he desired to serve him no matter how challenging that might be. These other monks, on the other hand, wanted to do whatever pleased them.

One day they plotted against Benedict by poisoning a pitcher of wine set out for one of the meals. When the saint raised his hand to bless the meal, however, the pitcher of wine broke. The saint knew immediately why it had broken, and was sad. He forgave the monks, but told them to change their hearts. He then returned to his cave in Subiaco. Saint Benedict loved the solitary life, for it allowed him to communicate with God and to come to a deeper knowledge of himself.

The Building of Twelve Monasteries

After returning to his cave, Saint Benedict discovered that he could no longer live there by himself. So many men had come to him that it was now time to build his own monasteries in order to accommodate all of those seeking the monastic life. He built twelve monasteries near the cave where he had begun his life as a hermit. This scene depicts one of those monasteries being built. Next to Saint Benedict is a monk holding a box of twelve architectural scrolls, representing the twelve monasteries he built.

In each of these monasteries there were at least twelve monks. Under Benedict's guidance they spent their days alternating between praying the Divine Office and doing the many kinds of work that are necessary to maintain a monastery. "Work and pray", *ora et labora*, was their motto.

Saint Benedict Recovers an Iron Blade from the Water

While one of the monks was clearing brush near the lake, the blade of his scythe came off and fell into the deepest part of the water. The monk immediately went to one of Benedict's most trusted disciples, Maurus, to ask forgiveness for his carelessness in losing a valuable tool. Maurus, who was aware of Benedict's holiness and his gift of working miracles, informed the saint of what had happened. Benedict said a prayer and, imitating the prophet Elisha, took the wooden handle and inserted the tip into the water. As in the Bible (2 Kings 6:6), the blade came to the surface and reattached itself to the handle. Saint Benedict then handed the scythe back to the astonished monk, who returned happily to his work.

Saint Maurus Saves Saint Placidus

Saint Benedict had two young disciples named Maurus and Placidus, sons of Roman noblemen who had come to live in the monastery and learn from the saint. This picture shows the scene from the life of Saint Benedict when Placidus went out to fetch some water from the lake. He carelessly dipped the bucket into the water, slipped, and fell into the lake. The current carried him about a stone's throw from the shore.

Even though he hadn't seen what happened with his own eyes, Benedict immediately felt that the boy was in danger. He then said to Maurus: "Run, Brother Maurus, because the boy who went to get water has fallen into the lake and is in grave danger of drowning." Maurus received a blessing from Benedict and then immediately ran out of the monastery toward the lake. When he got to the shore he just kept going, and because of his obedience to the saint's command, he was able to walk on the water as Saint Peter did in the Gospel. Thus the young Placidus was saved.

Saint Benedict and His Disciples Arrive at Monte Cassino

As Saint Benedict grew in holiness and wisdom his battles with the devil also began to increase. Eventually he moved from Subiaco to establish a monastery on the top of a mountain near the city of Cassino in southern Italy. This picture shows a scene from his life in which he and his disciples destroy an ancient pagan temple and altar dedicated to Apollo, and begin the construction of two chapels: one dedicated to Saint Martin and the other to Saint John the Baptist.

At this point in Benedict's life the devil would appear to him face to face, furious at the saint because of all the good he was doing for the salvation of souls. Nevertheless, Benedict, by the grace of Christ Jesus and his own determination, remained unafraid and steadfast in the ways of the Lord.

The Imaginary Kitchen Fire

While they were constructing the monastery, a bronze statue was found buried underground. The monks decided, for the time being, to place the idol in the kitchen. All of a sudden a blaze broke out so great that it seemed as though it was going to destroy the entire kitchen and perhaps the whole monastery. In haste, the monks got buckets of water to put out the flames. They kept throwing water onto the flames, yet the fire only increased. On hearing all the commotion, Saint Benedict arrived in the kitchen to see what was happening. He immediately understood what was going on. The fire was in their imagination; it was a deception of the devil to make it seem as though the bronze idol had power. The saint prayed, and the monks' eyes were opened to what was really going on: there was no real fire, no reason to panic. They had splashed water all over the kitchen for nothing!

The Meeting with King Totila

This picture shows Totila, king of the Goths, coming to pay homage to Saint Benedict. King Totila was near Monte Cassino on a military excursion, and while in the area he heard of the saintly life of Benedict. Before going to visit Benedict in person, he sent his shield-bearer Riggo to play a trick on the saint. Totila had Riggo dressed in his own royal clothes and escorted by his own men to the monastery where Benedict and his monks lived. The king thought that if Benedict was really what people said he was, then he should be able to know that Riggo was in fact an imposter and not the actual king.

No sooner had Riggo arrived at the monastery than Benedict directed him to take off the king's clothes, for he was not the king. Finally the real king arrived to pay homage, knowing that truly Benedict was what people said he was, a prophet and a man of God.

As soon as Totila saw Benedict he prostrated himself on the ground and would not get up. Saint Benedict went over to him to raise him up. During this encounter Saint Benedict prophesied to King Totila about his death, and exhorted him not to be so cruel.

A Monk Leaves the Monastery and Meets a Dragon

One of the monks decided to abandon the monastery. Saint Benedict begged him not to leave, but the monk left anyway. No sooner had he departed than he encountered a huge dragon on the road. Immediately seized by fear, he ran back to the monastery yelling that a dragon was trying to eat him alive! The other monks came out to help, but none of them saw the dragon, only the one who was trying to leave.

At Saint Benedict's prayer, it was given to this monk to see, in the form of a dragon, that he had been following the wrong path. After this event he promised not to leave, and he was faithful to God for the rest of his days.

Saint Benedict Raises a Young Boy from the Dead

In this picture we see Saint Benedict praying over a boy whom he had just raised from the dead. Benedict was returning from work in the fields when he encountered a man asking him to give back his son. Benedict did not understand, because the boy was not one of his monks, but Benedict soon found out what he meant. The father of this boy had carried his son's body to the entrance of the monastery with the hope that the saint would be able to bring him back to life. Benedict did not think that he should attempt such a miracle. He knew that only great saints like the apostles could make the dead rise. The father, being immovable, said he would not leave until Benedict brought his child back to life.

Saint Benedict then knelt and prayed: "O Lord, do not look upon my sins, but on the faith of this man, who pleads for the resurrection of his son, and restore to this body the soul which you took from it." No sooner had Benedict finished this prayer than the boy was restored to life and was given back to his father. Everyone rejoiced in the miracle the Lord God had granted by means of Saint Benedict's prayer!

The Miracle of His Sister Saint Scholastica

This picture shows the last time Saints Benedict and Scholastica saw each other on earth. Saint Gregory tells us that they used to meet each other at least once a year. Before their last encounter happened just down the mountain from the monastery of Monte Cassino, God had told Scholastica that her time on earth was short and that she would not live to see her brother again. When night fell, she begged Benedict not to go, but he insisted that he should leave, for it was time to go back to his monastery on top of the mountain. Scholastica so loved her brother that she wanted to spend the rest of the night conversing with him about God and the heavenly life.

Benedict's mind was made up: he was leaving! Remembering Saint John's words that "God is love" (1 John 4:8), his twin sister put her head down and humbly put her desire in God's hands. As soon as she lifted up her head a huge storm broke out, with thunder, lightning, and torrential rain, which made it impossible for Benedict to climb back up the mountain. The two then spent the rest of the night in holy conversation and prayer. The next day they went back to their respective monasteries.

The Death of His Sister Scholastica

Some three days after the encounter with Scholastica, Saint Benedict received the gift of knowing that his sister had just died. From his cell window he saw her soul going up to heaven in the form of a dove. Saint Gregory tells us that Saint Benedict rejoiced and was not sad at her death. His sister was now entering eternal life, where she would be perfectly happy with God. Knowing this, Benedict praised God and requested to have his sister's body brought up the mountain to his monastery. He had her body placed in the same tomb that he had prepared for himself. Thus, as their souls were united in God while they lived, they would also lie in the same tomb together.

The Death of Saint Benedict

Saint Gregory tells us that Benedict knew the exact day that he would die. He even announced it to some of his disciples. Six days before, he requested his tomb to be opened. Then his sickness continued to worsen. On the day of his death he had some of his monks bring him into the chapel so that he could receive the precious Body and Blood of the Lord Jesus Christ in the Eucharist. He was so sick that his disciples had to hold him up by his arms. Saint Benedict died standing, just after raising his hands to heaven and praying to God.

This picture shows a vision that two of his monks had. They saw Saint Benedict walking up to heaven on a carpeted path lined with shining lamps. The angelic figures represent the different choirs of angels.

Benedict's life, memory, and Rule remain with us to this day through hundreds of thousands of priests, monks, nuns, and lay people who have been inspired by his works.

A Prayer for the Intercession of Saint Benedict

Raise up in your Church, O Lord,
the spirit with which our holy father Saint Benedict was animated,
so that filled with the same spirit,
we may strive to love what he loved and to practice what he taught.
Through Christ our Lord,

Amen.

GLOSSARY

Abbot: The leader of a group of monks. The leader of a group of nuns is an abbess.

Cell: The bedroom of a monk.

Consecrated Life: The life given completely to God, as in the case of a priest, a monk, or a nun.

Divine Office: The hours of formal prayer observed by monks, nuns, and priests. These prayers are mainly composed of the psalms found in the Bible.

Gospel: The Greek word meaning "good news". When it begins with a small "g", it refers to the good news that Jesus makes us children of God. With a big "G" it means one of the four chapters in the Bible about the life of Jesus: Matthew, Mark, Luke, or John.

Habit: The special clothing worn by a monk or a nun.

Hermit: A monk who spends a great part of his life in solitude.

Hermitage: The place where the hermit lives.

Idol: A statue that is worshiped as if it were God, as if it had the power that belongs only to God.

Monastery: The place where monks or nuns live. Certain monasteries are known as abbeys.

Pagan: In the 5th century Europe, a non-Christian person who most likely worshiped ancient Roman gods and goddesses.

Penance: A prayer or an action that helps us to undo the damage done to ourselves by our sins.

Rule of Saint Benedict: A way of life for monks and nuns written by St. Benedict in the 5th century. The rule is so well known that many priests and lay people also use it for their everyday lives.